An Outcry Of Words

Edited by

Becki Mee

First published in Great Britain in 1999 by
POETRY NOW
Remus House, Coltsfoot Drive,
Woodston, Peterborough
PE2 9JX
Telephone (01733) 898101
Fax (01733) 313524

HB ISBN 0 75430 618 6
SB ISBN 0 75430 619 4

FOREWORD

Although we are a nation of poetry writers we are accused of not reading poetry and not buying poetry books: after many years of listening to the incessant gripes of poetry publishers, I can only assume that the books they publish, in general, are books that most people do not want to read.

Poetry should not be obscure, introverted, and as cryptic as a crossword puzzle: it is the poet's duty to reach out and embrace the world.

The world owes the poet nothing and we should not be expected to dig and delve into a rambling discourse searching for some inner meaning.

The reason we write poetry (and almost all of us do) is because we want to communicate: an ideal; an idea; or a specific feeling.

Poetry is as essential in communication, as a letter; a radio; a telephone, and the main criteria for selecting the poems in this anthology is very simple: they communicate.

CONTENTS

THE FLEA

Yesterday whilst having tea
I met a very friendly flea.
He said his name was Billy Blogg
and lived upon my silly dog.

He talked of this he talked of that
he talked of moving to my cat.
Just when I thought he was my friend
he bit me, and, well that's the end.

Les Young

WANTED MORE

With the new year
that so often comes
you think of the
old year that's gone
then you wanted more
but were short-changed
nineteen ninety nine is
the year, after that
it is the year
two thousand such an
enormous number for us
to have to deal with
anything new is hard
to come to any
strict terms with and
to understand each day
it's more than money
more than just taking
more to have now
that's no way for
us ever to have.

Richard Clewlow

REFLECTIONS

(For Brenda, my wife)

Quiet are the moments
Just before the dawn
Slowly fade the shadows
Where fantasies are born.

I lie awake still sleepy -eyed
Waiting for the sun
Reflecting on my life today
Things I've left undone.

It seems not very long ago
I could conquer all the world
From rags to riches I would go
As my future life unfurled.

But as my destiny unfolded
Here I lie today
Not rich, or famous, just ordinary
Yet content to be this way.

Because I have a home and children
Good health, I can't complain
A wife I love so very much
Who shares my joy and pain.

I thank God for the life he's given me
In all I do and say
I hope the future's just as good
As I reflect on life today.

GIG

THE TALE SPINNER

He talks about a creature,
He glorified an ant,
He tells about some feature,
That's found within a plant.

'Having left the orchid bell,
With stickers on its brow,
Inside its chosen ovule -
The membrane bends right down;
If the bee was heavier,
The shoot would bend too low,
And if it was much lighter,
A new plant would not grow.

Precisely when this timing,
They both became aware,
I cannot be aspiring,
They felt the need to share;
One hundred, maybe fifty,
Million years I cannot tell,
The bee was actually ready,
Attracted by the smell'

'Your view of graduation,
With good sense - I cannot agree!
Against the marvels of creation . . .
It's nonsense can't you see?
Fifty million (years) as a variable -
Too much, ifs, buts, and perhaps!
Why does it bend me double?
It's a joke - a ridiculous lapse!

'But if for promulgation,
The orchid needs the bee,
And both without creation,
Arrived spontaneously . . .
Such evolution incumbent,
On a billion other marks -
Surely makes redundant,
A Creator and all his works!

Tom Ritchie

TODAY ENGLAND IS FREE

But for this lovely freedom, we owe this to a super, great man.
He knew in advance the danger that was to face England.
But more to the point the Queen knew too well that he was,
at the time, the only man to save England from the slavery
of the madman. The dictators and the tyrants.
He did not only save England, but Europe as well from
the slavery of Hitler.
If the Queen had not called him, today we would not enjoy
the liberty and the freedom that the English people love so much.
Thank you to the great man that made England free
from any dictators and tyrants.
England survived all the difficulties of the war time.
The war was a grave one but because the super man knew everything
in advance he always had the advantage.
He was very intelligent and he planned well
to have the upper hand at all times.
England should always remember his name and his talent.
We still enjoy the good living and the prosperity.
He changed England's destiny.
Because of his super ability he made a new history.
He could see the future of England and Europe too,
well in advance of the time.
I salute the super, great man.
Long live his name and England.

Antonio Martorelli

ROUND THE WORLD BALLOON TRIP, DECEMBER 1998!

Richard Branson flew up in the air
In his big balloon, with his blue eyes and blond hair!

He started from Morocco
      then
through a 'corridor'
      between Iran and Russia!

Once over the Chinese Border
      the balloon hits the desolate
      Tibetan plateau!

So, Steve Fossett,
      Per Lindstrom
      and Richard Branson
had to change course to avoid Iraq,
      and wait for China's decision!

With red flames a-flaming
and the balloon now enlarging!

Up they went full of
      anticipation and excitement!

On Christmas day Honolulu, Hawaii!

A seven-day trip!

Over Everest and Tibet!

Marie Barker

HAIL FELLOW WELL MET

'Well, old friend, nice to see you again,
You're looking well. How's the family? - Good.
A pity you didn't call as you said you would,
But you haven't changed an inch; hey! That
Belt's starting to pinch and your chin's
Grown a double beneath.' And we laugh together
Over relived pranks forever a joy;
And briefly the flame that wrought us young men
Burns true in our middle-aged eyes.
Then it dies and you must be on your way:
'Nice seeing you,' you say with an unctuous lie,
To which I smile and wonder where you
Got the guile and shallowness for sham,
Where in the boyhood friend was such
A hopeless little man. You say all the right things
That no one believes, yet you've more friends
Than anyone needs; and drinking cronies too
For when you're all blue because inside
Your lonely heart bleeds. I feel sorry for you,
Dear friend I once knew, sorry you took this path,
For life's journey is sad enough when all's right,
And sadder still when friendships don't last.

Peter Waverly

My Mother

From my earliest days and in my youth,
you have always been there, to show me the truth,
you nurtured me, and you held my hand,
with faltered steps, you helped me stand,
when I would fall, you would steady me,
when not understanding, you'd help me to see,
when I was hurt, and in a child's pain,
you were always there, to take the strain,
as I grew up, you helped me to learn,
for when I would later work and earn,
you taught me life's truths, and of what is right,
and when I was wrong, I felt your might,
of all the women, on God's green earth,
I thank you Mother, for giving me birth,
I thank you for showing me the right way,
and of your love, I simply must say,
because of you, I have flown so high,
I've reached the clouds, and I've touched the sky,
I have travelled the world, I have nurtured fame,
you gave me life, and you gave me my name,
I love and adore you - above any other,
for you are, always and will be, my mother.

James F Woodard

WHY!

Golden-haired little girl who brought us laughter and joy
And in her passing left behind great sadness and weeping
Time has now deadened those memories but can never erase
Treasured thoughts of our loved one now quietly sleeping

Those photographs, toys, the simple trinkets of children
Were enshrined for that grief passing years have now mended
Briefly she flourished only to vanish as a summertime mist
God's love queried for this young life so capriciously ended

For the loved ones who bore her their heartbreak is stilled
As they now both lie by her side reunited forever in peace
But for us memories still linger though diminished by time
Which will in turn claim us all and they will finally cease

M F Base

WHERE'S THE TOWN CENTRE?

You cannot find Great Witley.
You search with all your might.
It came out in the open once
then dodged back out of sight.

The roads go racing past it.
The signposts are a joke,
and don't go asking people
they're an awkward lot of folk.

Nearby they have a famous church
where spirits whinge and whine.
They thought they'd reached Great Witley but
they never crossed the line.

There also is a Witley Court,
the grass once overrun it.
It cost a bomb, went up in smoke,
and nob'dy knows who done it!

There is this Inn called Hundred House,
you'll find it on the map.
King Charles once had a pint here with
his head stuck on his lap.

I think this place, Great Witley,
is houses that were spilt
by all surrounding neighbours
on a town they never built,

So don't go searching for it,
try Stourport instead.
Ten minutes here you'll say 'My Lord
I wish I'd stopped in bed.'

Leonard Jeffries

CHARACTERS 'I KNEW'

The 'shipyard' was a noteworthy place to see,
Many types of characters, of our humanity.
The skills of our tradesmen were first class,
British ships were built to last.
But, many of our characters, of years long past,
A young blacksmith with blisters on his hand,
Treated them by weeing on his hands.
One labourer had a similar plan,
To remove dirty oil, off his hands,
He washed them clean, with his warm wee,
Before he went, to make his foreman's tea.
One labourer would sit, and Vim his false teeth,
Another would pluck hairs from his cheek.
Yet, jobs they had the capability to do,
They felt it was a honour to do.
The toilet block, was a dirty chore,
Yet you could eat a meal, off that floor.
Our shipyards are no longer here,
But what would we ever do,
With our characters who worked with me and you . . .

Brian Marshall

In My Views

State what you see
Put it down in writing
If poet you wish to be
You may not be a Burns,
Keats or Byron,
Yet those things in life you
See, mountains, streams
A tree
Pit patter of tiny feet
Childish laughter such a treat
Try to stir the human soul
Make someone smile
Laugh, or perhaps make someone sad
Don't write trash
Poetry's not about cash
Be truthful in what you write
If all these things one can do
Perhaps one day a poet they may call you.

B Croft

BODY POSITIVE

Life, death!

Floods me, goads me,
Leads me beside hot beaches
Where I run, a dazzling sea
Cheering me on, and I wonder
Where the lark has gone
That fixed me with its cheer
Before abandoning me here
Like a forgotten toy
Filled with the joy of its
Having played me out
Before going about
Nature's own
Business

Life, death!

Calls me, galls me,
Urges me back, back to you;
But we are gone, the taste of us
Honey on my tongue
Where we romped and played
Like tots in make-believe
Heading barefoot among jellyfish
For the Punch and Judy man
Who'll make us laugh
If anyone can
Before the sun goes down
And our time
Forgotten

Life, death!

Overtaken us now, beckoning;
I'll not rush my pace, for
We already ran our race, won
A place among these stars
Enchanting this lulling swell.
All's well; one lost toy recovered
And taken home, Punch and Judy
In a packing case sleeping it off
At some bed and breakfast;
I, filled with such a night
Far exquisite for words
Like those we shared
Before AIDS

R N Taber

THE SIN OF OMISSION

It isn't the things you do
It's the things you leave undone
Which gives you a bit of heartache
At the setting of the sun
The tender word forgotten
The letter you did not write
The flower you might have sent
Are your haunting ghosts tonight
The stone you might have lifted
Out of a brother's way
The bit of heartsome counsel
You were hurried too much to say
The loving touch of the hand
The gentle and winsome tone
That you had no time or thought for
With troubles enough of your own
The little acts of kindness
So easily out of mind
Those changes to be helpful
Which everyone may find

William Price

ENID

We met occasionally
for a nice break.
Fresh coffee, hot toast
and salady things.
Flowers were sent
and poems were read.
What are phones for
but to communicate
the tenderest of things?
A robin sits
shivering and shaking
under the heavy sky.
Numbness disappears
when the rain
makes a heavy din.
Come red bird
and let us unite,
there are songs
to sing
this Christmas night.

Tom Clarke

COLD, LOST, TIRED AND BROKEN

So cold
I shiver
Where the sun
May never enter in
And darkness wraps
Her heavy blanket round

So lost
I wander
Through a subterranean
Dank maze
Where the only noise
Is my own heartbeat's pound

So tired
Yet my instincts tell me
'Move along,
Don't sleep'
I can feel the breath
Of trouble close behind

So broken
Is my spirit
Overburdened with the past
Every step a pain
That keeps me here
Confined

Kim Montia

HIGHLAND LONGING

They long to dance the Highland Fling,
To wear the tartan right way round.
The swords they cross, the bells they sing
And no one's severed toes were found.

To wear the tartan right way round
For Gordon's Gay, less common lays,
And no one's severed toes were found,
In haggis piped in, all its ways.

For Gordon's Gay, less common lays,
The Forest Flowers wilted soon
As evening fell and tired feet
Sluggish, spring to life and leap -
The fingers flew. The pipes, they peep.

As evening fell, and tired feet
Tried to keep up with every move,
The fingers flew, the pipes they peep
And curious whispers filled the floor.

Tried to keep up with every move
Of tapping tendons to the tune,
And curious whispers filled the floor
To swallow up the New Year moon.

Of tapping tendons to the tune,
The swords they cross the bells they sing,
Wants satisfied for now, but soon
They long to dance the Highland Fling.

Diane Burrow

HOPE

It doesn't make a difference if we're black or white,
we're all one in God's eyes!
Just because we're on different sides of the road,
doesn't mean we're not all equal!
I see you as a white person.
You see me as a black person!
But that doesn't mean
that you and I can't be friends!

A person once said to me 'What is your wish?'
I would say something like, 'I want a pony.'
That person would say 'That's funny because
all I want is peace around the world.'
I think to myself that's a pretty silly wish!
But when I thought about it, I thought to myself,
everybody probably wishes that!

I'm not aware of too many things,
but I'm pretty much aware of the things
that go on in my neighbourhood.
Are you aware of what goes on in your neighbourhood?

Rachel Henningham

SOMEONE TO LOVE

There is someone special for each of us,
Someone to laugh with, someone to cuss,
A pair of lips to kiss you and arms to hold you tight,
Someone to keep you warm on a cold night,
A loving smile and a look that says it all,
Loving words that make you feel ten feet tall,
Always there throughout the night and day,
Through thick and thin come what may,
That special someone who says I love you,
Someone special who helps you come through,
Together your love will keep you strong,
Facing whatever life brings along,
Safe in the knowledge of your love for each other,
Always being there for one and another,
Remember when life gets a bit too tough,
There is someone special for each of us.

Sandy Grebby

THE RAILWAY STATION

One day I missed a train
It left me standing cold.
I waited for the next
Near to a man very old.

He asked me for the time
I grunted my reply
He smiled and said these words
'I see anger in your eye.

I saw you miss that train.
Whose fault? Well it's your own.
Your temper flows from you
You should have stayed at home.'

I laughed at his repose.
His style and stance was bland
'How dare you sneer at me!
You're too old to understand.'

He turned full square on me.
'My boy, I may be old
Yet life has taught me well
And I am not standing, cold.'

Peter Mitchell

GHOSTS OF THE SCREEN

Ghosts:
those gorgeous young men on TV
just try to reach out to them, and you will see . . .
they make girls' hearts beat, and they give them beliefs
as they work their profession as soul-robbing thieves:

write them a letter as one to one
and there's more chance of a reply from God's son;
and if you bump into one by pure chance
you won't know it happened, for he'll trick you askance!

yet they're made of material, but they're just not there
for they hide behind screens, and no one knows where . . .
unless you happen to belong to the world of ghosts,
for then they'll materialise, and call you the most . . .

. . . they do this to each other all the time
as each one tries to social climb
further into his world of electron screens
to try to become the ghost of the biggest means . . .

Tricia Nolan

VYRNWY

Apple green
Mists upon a mirror
With
Stalks of ivy blue,
Slender
With the brush strokes
Of
December too;
Ripples
Upon the wild wind
The waters
Are calling home,
Banks
Of holding ochre
Fall into
Beds of winter's dream;
As autumn golds
Have folded
Leaving
No witness to the scene.

Romansky

A YEAR OF FULFILMENT

I wrote throughout my childhood, but the need
To earn a living stole upon the scene
And, falsely urging caution then, would lead

Me into shelving my main aims, and mean
A life of work in a related field
Until its sad decline would intervene.

At first my chosen way appeared to yield
Due satisfaction in a worthwhile cause,
But then destructive forces start to wield

Their hollow weapons, whose blunt use ignores
Those proven values, standards and the modes
Of working on which true achievement draws.

Price-cutting, modernising are the goads
Now used to wear down consciences of those
Objecting as sheer nonsense makes inroads.

As the revolt of reason ever grows,
The order comes: 'Do more with less; replace
Old principles with new; do not oppose.'

To do things thoroughly denies the pace
Of modern life: make do and muddle through
And superficialize, though you debase.

Impossible this damage to undo,
So it was time to leave the field, and spend
Fulfillingly the years that would ensue.

Exasperations I can now transcend,
Engage in tasks more meaningful at last,
And give to writing what I did intend.

To more rewarding work I now hold fast -
This year's enjoyment has been truly vast!

Anne Sanderson

1998 CHRONICLE

(Dedicated to Akhtar Eqbal)

1998 became for me very suddenly sad,
one of my gloomiest, upsetting, darkest
years in my life for ever
of every moment's every days
kaleidoscopic life's livings.

I know I have to die
the time, the date, the day, the year
unknown to me as yet.

So I was aware,
my brothers will die one day in due course
but not so suddenly, so quickly,
he is the eldest the number one
of my parents, my only brother.
The youngest I am
with a sister after me

It's my hard luck
that I did not pray for God's approval
and as well as informed my brother
what was my intention,
what was going on in my mind
that I was planning.
I was hoping to bring you to London
to have a glimpse of the city
and then enquire
what do you consider this place
where you kindly, lovingly set me to study.
May his soul rest in peace

Amen.

Ghazanfer Eqbal

A Girl Name 'C'

I met dear, sweet, loving 'C'
While developing myself at Timehri
She was short, thick and sweet
With all the qualities for a delightful treat.

Oh! 'C' what have you done to me?
Why cause me so much misery?
In my nightly dreams only you I see
I was once happy and carefree,
Like a bomb you exploded and destabilised me.

I fell for you without a doubt
With a few kisses you won the bout
You caught me cold I didn't stand a chance
Headlong I plunged into a brief romance.

I had to leave against my will
Sweet memories revive your magic thrill
Your soft voice, your gentle touch
Those little things mean very much.

Now I am here and you are there
You act as if you do not care
Did you mean all those loving words you spoke?
Or were they part of your funny joke?

And should we never meet again
Time will surely ease the pain
Whatever I do, where ever I'll be
I'll always remember sweet, loving 'C'.

Omald Bakker

LOVE'S OFFERING

'Each year he planted them'

For her,
He sowed them,
One long rank
Along the garden path.
Shallots, spiky green,
Spread out behind.
Parsley, aromatic thyme
And pungent sage
Skirted the edges.

From rounded spheres
Of dusty brown
Green shoots, almost translucent cane;
Piercing their way
Through the sun-warmed earth.

He stickered the earth
With hazel branches, he'd chosen
As he lay his farm-hedges.
This year they'd be decked
With scented sweet peas
Not dancing lamb's-tails.

Tendrils clung tenaciously
To their roughened surface
Each pea climbed, felt for support,
Blossomed in pinks and vermilions,
Purples and white, creams fluted and frilled
Stickers left over were placed by the hedge
Enticing the blackbirds to nest.

He'd pick the first blooms for her
I see him still
Walking indoors bunched offering held out
In work-scarred hand.
Love's token for her

Helen Perry

LIFE'S LAW

Pregnancy sorrow, pregnancy joy,
Will it be girl or will it be boy?
Some babies are wanted, some are not.
Some loved a little, some loved a lot.
Some will grow happy, some will grow sad,
Some will grow good, and some will grow bad.
Some will be rich, but some will be poor,
Quite a few in trouble with the law.
Unwanted can grow to be much loved,
But some are trained with a hand ungloved.
Silver-spooned babies can turn out wrong,
Runts of family can turn out strong.
Some put their brains to very good use,
Some kids suffer a lot of abuse.
Why can't they all be brought up with love.
The world will show them the push and shove.
They're born unasked, into this life hurled.
Too soon they're lost out into the world.
Though some their life will end much too soon,
To some children that would be a boon.
Some make life happy, some make life sad,
Some make it good, but some make it bad.
Some will get rich, and some will be poor,
All we can do is try, that's Life's Law.

N A Thomas

THE SEA

I talk to the sea
It creeps up and touches me
Washes over, cleanses, soothes
With its ever-changing moods
Takes my worries one by one
With every wave and swell brings calm
So very strong, so deep, so tall
Making me feel so very small
Troubles gone; too much to hope
With its help I know I'll cope
Nothing ever stays the same
To and fro, rough and tame
So life seems to race along
I must not write it off as wrong
It is just the sea of life
Accept it as it is
Ever surging, rushing, rolling
Till the end of time.

Mary Alison

DESPAIR

My eyes are opened, and like a black-coiled cat
I squirm and the hell begins.
I close them firm to think of fresh things, but all are trouble-dashed
As early demons mount once more
Like spiralling cilia transporting havoc,
Beating in rhythm to the brain which swells and swirls
Pulsing damned images of danger, forever to be fought.

Worse than yesterday, heavy brushstrokes of black-green waves
Smear against a helpless, twitching, rope-laddered hull.
Shiny-smooth brown banisters descend forever
Into a hopeless hollow.
A forbidding red-brick well, a slimy vortex
Of rounded dark unknown, inviting terror.
Heaving blurs of aching water deep
And a bridge rail wide enough to sit upon.

My eyes come alive and my neck twists, legs and arms tense tendrils.
All the parts I cannot feel jump and writhe to distract
And offer hope that this will die for just a little while.
Breaks then another nauseous wave from the very bowels
As I try to sink and escape the pest
Clutching at furniture that unfocused, won't stand still.
Gnawed by music that won't be controlled.
Can this be my brain? Natural mischief or ungodly possession?

My eyes are closed and summon a curtain of blackness
That surely no devil can disturb or penetrate.
Then an unexpected tremor, and baleful panic grips my breast
And I am hideous with fear.
What precious imagination unrequired!
A knot of string pulls from the very core of my giddy head.
Confused as a kaleidoscope, my jungled stomach rolls alive and reels
Away from reality.

Whatever was real?
I recall people who spoke to me,
Tired noises of a normal day, playing in the blue air.
Pictures, smells and tastes. Gone. None of these sweet ghosts live here
Except in images that perhaps breathed long ago.
The bite returns, I scuttle back to the abyss.
A spasm sends a cry to touch the world, no longer there.
So I stare at the ceiling and say I'll bear it. The worst will soon be gone.
I swear, and clench my fists and strain
Against that which brushstrokes would never dare create.
And await the next ebb and flow
Of despair.

John Daniels

HIS BIRTHDAY

It's the birthday of our friend, my dears,
No time for loneliness or tears,
For He's our brother, helper, friend
Faithful, abiding, 'til the end . . .

In pastures new, then, He will say
'I walked beside you all the way
My loving hand erased your tears
My soothing voice allayed your fears . . .

E'en now I enter darkened heart
Spreading My sunlight . . . see it dart . . .
Into every yearning soul
Scattering misery, grief and woe . . .
Yes, it's My birthday - come, celebrate,
Turn to Me . . . for it's never too late
To be held in your Saviour's gentle arms
Lulling, forever, anguished alarms . . .
Healer, brother, shepherd, friend,
You see, My titles have no end . . .
Turn to Me this Christmas-tide
Constant companion whate'er betide . . .
Then, when this season's come and gone
Still My presence shall linger on
Filling your heart with light from above
Filling your soul with My peace and love!'

Anne R Way

THE ECLIPSE

Young and carefree except for our study
Students we were, some serious, some funny
In our hands were pieces of broken glass
Crowds had collected, they let us pass.

The sun rose that morning as it always did
Obeying laws of nature as it was bid
In a short time it would vanish from sight
Consternation then we would be without light.

It seemed the whole city was gathered there
Waiting expectantly, wonders to share
Scarcely believing it would come about
It did of course of this we had no doubt.

Gracefully gliding like the lady she was
Not shining now, just a shadow to pass
Night descended on the park at noon
Leicester obliterated by the moon.

We were not blinded by the vision we saw
Knowing quite well what smoked glass was for
The next eclipse many decades away
All wondering would we see that day?

Evelyn Sharman

MESSINES RIDGE

They advanced together side by side
the orange and the green
together they fought and died
amidst that awful battle scene

The cream of Ireland north and south
bridged the gulf divide
at Messines Ridge they sacrificed
to stem war's evil tide

The cream of Ireland advanced again
but this time not in war
again with pride they bridged the gulf
to build the Irish tower

The tower at Messines stands high and proud
a remembrance of war and peace
the terrible conflict that war brings
and that all wars may cease

Frank Scott

LOVE STRIKES

When love strikes you from above there's nothing you can do.
I've been hit like a tidal wave. I'm wet right through.

I wasn't looking for love. It just shined down on me.
Now I'm blinded and I just can't see.

I'm caught like a rabbit in a trap. I'm not going to try and break free.
I'm going to wait for you to come and rescue me.

I was on top of a cliff. Didn't know what was below.
A strange mist came over me and I just let go.

Deeper and deeper I was falling. But I just didn't care.
When you're in love you can just fly through the air.

Love makes you look at things in a different light.
When you're in the darkest place everything seems so bright.

Brett Ireland

MY BEACH TREE

I have a beach tree by my front gate,
the falling of the leaves cover my garden and lawns,
making a lot of work cleaning them away.
Prince Charles talks to plants and trees, so I decided to talk to this one,
I said 'You're standing there, so tall and strong,
in the place where you belong,
they planted you, pleasure to give,
but why did it have to be, just where I live!
I know you shade me from the sun,
and squirrels up and down you run,
but please, oh please, give thought to me,
when you drop your leaves for me to see,
don't you realise the work you cause,
when clapping your branches in applause,
you may be happy - but no not me,
when you shed your leaves - *dear me tree!*
I have to collect them all the time,
they are yours, you know - not mine.'
He's not listened to a word I have said,
he's standing there shaking his head,
oh well, the night and day will pass,
once more I'll have to clear my grass.

A E Steer

THEN

Drinking lager's
cool
remember
me from
school?
Sat alone
in the corner
looking at you.
We met alone
on some island
blood, fish and
bone
I loved you
more than water
stood guessing
and alone.

P Allen

BALLAD OF THE EVERYDAY PEOPLE

Could have been a painter
Laid out all over a canvas
The way I see this world
Instead I'm what I am
Just an ordinary, working class type
Just an ordinary, everyday man
Could have been a poet
Spread out in meaningful verses
The way I feel about life
Instead I'm what you see
Just an ordinary, everyday man
Just ordinary, plain old me
But my love is very special
And it should express more than words
How I feel about you here
No words could ever be enough
No song could be beautiful enough
For a heart so plain, so clear
Other people don't mind
Sharing their world outlooks
The world's sorted out every Friday
On Monday it's back in bits
Just an ordinary bunch of people
Just an ordinary world that slips
Could have been a hero
Spreading world peace with a song
By touching people's souls
Instead I'm where I am
Stuck in the middle of nowhere
Just an ordinary, everyday man

Rodger Moir

SOLUTIONS

Leaf on a branch wilts then falls
Like diminished love, colourless and torn
Playground of life, tumbles occur
Ups and downs a-many, life also sends
Unaware, unwarranted circumstances end
Solutions optional why pretend.

Alan Jones

BROKEN PROMISES

We all make resolutions
With fervour and with haste
As the old year fades away
And a new one takes its place.

On a diet I will go
I'm going to give up smoking
I'll make a start tomorrow
Oh! You think I'm only joking.

I'll not shout at the kids
And I'll wash the car on Sundays
Keep the garage free from junk
And walk the dogs - well some days.

I'll smile at all the strangers
That I meet upon my way
I'll not get cross when in a queue
And on time the bills I'll pay.

I will remember Connor's birthday
And presents I will send
Instead of throwing out the socks
The holes I'll sit and mend.

These promises I mean to keep
When tomorrow starts anew
But please remember to forgive me
If I break just one or two.

Pamala Girdlestone

EVERY YEAR THE SAME

Every day I'll dust the ornaments
Every day I'll clean the bath
Every day I'll wipe the skirting board
Every day I'll sweep the path

Every day I'll write some poetry
Every day I'll read some Greek
Every day I'll take some exercise
Every day I'll learn to speak

Every day I'll do some gardening
Every day I'll rake the lawn
Every day I'll do the ironing
Every day I'll be up at dawn

Every year I am so resolute
Every year I mean so well
Every year it never works -
I don't want each year a hell

P Wolstenholme

NEW YEAR'S RESOLUTION

If a new year's resolution had to be made by me, I would start at the top of the tree.

I would take all the members of parliament and the PM that would do for a start, I would sack all of them.

Then I would go to the ones with all the money, they would come down to bread without honey.

Then I would go to the poor, the infirm and the old, I would give them gas, electricity so they would not be cold.

Then I would give them honey to go on their bread, so they would now be warm, contented and fed.

Now if the National Lottery was run by me, there would be no giving it to the Arts or such.

No I would give it to the National Health Service, education, research or such.

Then if they made me a king for just one day, I would give all who need it a grand holiday.

I would not keep buying from Germany, Honk Kong or Japan, I would buy everything British that I can.

Then perhaps we could put the *great* back in Britain, then I could be proud of who I am. *English*, yes *English* that's what I am.

Loose my identity, by using foreign funny money, controlled by Brussels, I don't think that's funny.

If you ask all of the people what they want to be, they will say, they want to be *proud, English* and stay that way.

God save the Queen.

Ronald B Astbury

RESOLVE

I think I'll give up smoking. Yes, that's a good idea.
Though I've said it once before, about this time of year.
This time I really mean it. Just you wait and see.
Ninety nine and onwards will be a smokeless time for me.

The hours crawl so slowly. I've done this long enough.
What harm could there be in one more surreptitious puff?
And then I'll really mean it. Just you wait and see.
That last cigarette is all there'll be for me.

You know that I could do it, if I really wanted to.
For my strong willpower would surely get me through.
Next year I'll really do it. Just you wait and see.
I'll smoke no cigarettes in the next century.

M J Scutter

RESOLUTIONS

We stood together on the high cliff's dizzy edge.

'Now,' whispered the Voice within, 'The new year
Comes apace; renew those vows you owe;
Resolve again, breathe fire and heat,
That you'll not bow to tyranny and hate;
Appeal for adamantine strength, and more,
That you'll resist temptations sweet, and all
That pampers self, or panders to your body's
Baser needs. Be fierce as any cursed dog
To howl down hypocrites, who cannot see
The truth for lies; sink blood-soaked teeth
Into the wretched principles of enemies,
Who think only to promote themselves
Beneath the sickly guise of working
For the common weal.'
                          And such-like noble,
Zealous sentiments, declared this inner Voice.

Alas, oh Voice, too late. My feeble
Resolutions stand, like grandad's slippers
By the fire; they're worn familiar now by age
And constant use, and moulded into shape
By years of toil, and body's self-abuse.
My strongest resolution sinks
Into the weary weakness of my ageing will -
A pebble's ripples in a murky pond.

Oh, ancient Voice, enough. With me
You've stayed too long. Go seek another
To fulfil your dreams.
                          And that was all.
I stood awhile on the high cliff's dizzy edge,
Alone, and felt strange silence all around.

Jay Whittam

FOLLOW YOUR DREAMS

If you have a dream that's calling
let it carry you away,
don't be put off by people saying
you'll never have your way.
Because everyone is fighting
trying to be free,
not wanting to be held back
by what you should believe.

You've got to follow your dreams
be guided by the stars,
look around and inside yourself
and find out who you are.
You've got to trust in yourself
look for the light in you,
believe in what you want to and why
not because you've been told to.

Everyone has answers
that they all think are true,
they'll try to tell you 'they're right'
but it's really up to you.
You can conform to their way
follow them from now,
but you know the truth is in your heart,
and only you can show them how.

Suzanne Nicholls

TO BE CONTENT TO BE
(New Year's Resolution of an M E Sufferer)

I resolve to be content to be,
As God intended us as human beings,
And not to do, we are not human 'doings'!
To do too much will fuel this ME,
Prolong it, further limiting my doings,
Remember none of us are super-beings!

How can doing nothing bring content?
But can contentment grow from small beginnings?
Will God perhaps empower me through my 'nothings'?
To tolerate this illness am I meant
To understand the good in seeming 'nothings',
To offer thanks for chance of new beginnings?

Most are blessed with normal energy
And they in human terms present salvation,
As none of us can live in isolation,
But paradoxically with this M E
To be content to bear the isolation,
To rest in 'being', may be my salvation.

Put aside that life so full of care
And turn to God to make this resolution;
Away with busyness, away frustration;
Afflicted, I have time to lie and stare;
Let go, let God make good of my frustration
And give me strength to keep this resolution.

Janet C Forrest

OLD AND NEW YEAR

This is the time of year promises made
In times past, are revived and remembered.
Were they kept or forgotten is the question
In them did we fail or succeed,
Whatever memories of pain or happiness they hold
The expected or unexpected throughout the old year.

This is the time to renew resolutions old or new.
Then in twelve months hence we'll look back.
At those again we've kept or forgotten.
Only one really matters in the year ahead.
Ensure the one you love has the most
Enjoyable year they ever had.

John Bower

PROMISES PROMISES!

I once made a resolution to start slimming,
My good intentions nearly lasted for a day.
With chocolate cake I was soon sinning,
To celebrate my best friend's coming of age.

I even made a promise to stop drinking,
No more wine or brandy would I sup.
But my boyfriend ditched me leaving my spirits sinking,
And a pint of lager really cheered me up!

One year for a new car I started saving,
I really made the effort to raise the cash.
But for that slinky black dress I'd a craving,
Though expensive, in it I really cut a dash!

This year I'm going to start a revolution,
A promise to last more than just a week.
I'll be making no more new year's resolutions,
At least I know that is one promise I can keep!

B Eyre

PERFECT!

A New Year's Resolution,
But which one shall I choose?
I really am so perfect,
That there's nothing I can lose!

I am not a drinker,
So I cannot give up drink.
Cigarettes are voodoo,
As I cannot bear the stink!

I'm never know to gamble,
As I'm careful with my cash.
Bad language never leaves my lips,
As that's a little rash!

I never steal from anyone,
And always pay my due.
I do not lose my temper,
And frown on those who do!

I cannot give up chocolates,
Or sweets of any kind.
They're things I never fancy,
So are never on my mind!

I really am so perfect,
That I cannot think of any
New Year's Resolutions, but
I'm sure there must be many!

Oh, this is very difficult,
Am I such a *bore?*
Now *there's* a Resolution, so
I'll bore you all no more!

Rosalie A L Jackson

HERE WE GO AGAIN

It's December and here we go again
Deciding which - denied - will cause least pain.
Perhaps noxious nicotine or even demon drink
Renunciation of either can drive you to the brink.
Maybe overspending is your main fault
Those bank statements can give one quite a jolt.
One friend's problem is she's never on time
For in her bed she loves to recline.
An alarm clock with a raucous bell
Cured her of tardiness, it seems, very well.
Another friend's addiction is the phone
Sending or receiving - she can't leave it alone.
A male pal loves to gossip all day
(Most of his colleagues keep out of his way.)
My own downfall is a love of good food
A pastime to enjoy whatever my mood.
And as I make my resolve once more,
To forego the calories which I do so adore.
If I succeed my life will never be the same
But should I fail I know it's my willpower to blame!

Margaret Phillips

RESOLUTIONS

Be resolute and in your mind
Be firm. This way you'll find
Your actions will never waver
And right will conquer wrong.
Be resolute, but look before you leap.
For then you'll sense the errors 'ere you reach them,
That rise to break your resolutions
So thus it is, that you will win,
And over-ride the weakness from within.

Ivy Broomfield

RENAISSANCE

I will sweep it all aside
Disaster and hurt pride.
I will leave it all behind
Put it out of my mind.
I will make a fresh start,
Will ease my wounded heart
With actions of goodwill
To those who love me still.

Will it work, I ask
Is this difficult task
Too great for me
In my incompetency?

Can I honestly change?
It will be very strange
To re-jig my past.
This mood may not last.

But try it I will,
I'll endeavour to fill
Empty rooms of despair
With sunlight and air.

Christina Stowell

I'M ADDICTED!

It's easy for you to say,
Stop doing it right away.
I try so hard each day,
The need won't go away.

I've tried for so many years,
And shed so many tears.
So many worries and fears,
Make it hard to give up my dears.

I know you say you are choking,
Just because I am smoking.
With all your loving cajoling,
I really want to stop smoking.

Anna King

RESOLUTIONS

From '69 to '73, my resolution stated:
'I ain't gonna bite my nails no more' -
I dropped *that* one for '74 ...
From '74 to '78, my resolution stated:
'I'll write a book, when I have the time'.
I dropped *that* one for '79 ...
From '79 to '81, my resolution stated:
'I'll pay the bills the day they're due'.
Gave up hope on *that* for '82.

I made no resolutions from '82 to '88 -
But I managed to grow my nails quite long, albeit rather late!

From '89 to '94, my resolution stated:
'I'm going to pass my test to drive'.
Failed the fourth test attempt in '95 ...
From '95 to '98, the simplest resolution:
'I'm just gonna be the best wife I can'.
Best wasn't good enough, and off went my man.

So my resolution for '99 is one somewhat perverse -
Whatever it is I *want* to resolve, I'll resolve the *reverse!*

Sallie Copeland

RESOLUTIONS

We make them every year in a euphoric state
of mind after the celebrations of Christmas
and the New Year.
How long do we keep them, one week, two weeks . . . ?
No more resolutions for me, life is too short.
Having reached the age of indiscretion I mean to
enjoy what time I have left.
Olé.

Joyce Anlezark

RESOLUTIONS? WELL, JUST A FEW

This year I'll try not to;

Swear at drivers who don't indicate,
Curse any coaches that turn up late,
Swear at the rain when I have no brolly,
As I get soaked through and really soggy,
Curse rude people who think it's their right,
To have a door held open, and be impolite,
Curse the postman, when someone else's letter comes through the door,
And criticise his eyesight, which seems to be so poor,
Get annoyed when computers just don't want to work,
And wave my arms like a complete and utter berk,
Let certain people wind me up,
And treat me like their little pup,
Swear at cars when I try to cross the street,
So many bad, bad words that I just cannot repeat,
Curse bad weather on summer days out,
It really makes me swear and shout!
Swear when the video chews a tape,
Twisting it into a brand new shape,
Curse when the taxi fails to show,
Where on earth is it? We just don't know,
Swear when time is just flying away,
And I'm running late on a working day,
Curse when I manage to put down the phone,
Ending an earful of complaints and one long moan,
Swear when the toothpaste falls off my brush,
And drops in the sink as minty mush,

But it will be very difficult!

Stephen Norris

I RESOLVE ...

My breath is drawing tighter,
I'm paralysed with fear.
The day which I've been dreading,
Is very nearly here.

I've worried for a while,
Been getting little sleep.
I've promised resolutions,
Which I know I cannot keep.

The New Year's now upon us,
Nine hours, I've been strong.
But it's weakened my resistance,
And I know I can't last long.

Alas I find that I was right,
Temptation had her way.
Though I hope to have a second chance,
Come next New Year's day.

Louise Everitt

I'm Glad I Didn't

If I'd stuck to each New Year's resolution
That over the years I have made,
Life would have been so very boring,
Uneventful, unexciting and staid.

Norman Spence

AFTER TODAY

Today I will
> put the washing in the washing machine
> shop at the supermarket
> clean the carpets
> write a letter to my sister
> make soup
> weed a square yard of the garden

It is a full day today

Yesterday
> I did the same

That was a full day too

And tomorrow?
> I shall go to Spain
> stop a bullfight
> kiss passionately
> sing in some theatre
> dine conversationally
> avert a war
> see my publisher
> listen to the sap rising
> buy a small country house
> contribute to OXFAM
> kill somebody
> break for coffee with the cat
> read 'The Waves'
> wear strange clothes that suit me
> understand ageing

I must sleep well tonight

Rosamund Hall

MY NEW YEAR RESOLUTION

I've got to diet, it's not good, I've really got to slim,
Looking at me in the mirror, I go out more than I go in.
They tell me how to test the fat, to find if you've got too much,
Is to grab the blubber round your waist, that's if you can bear to touch.
If you can pinch an inch, they say, where your waistband should be put,
You're only slightly overweight, my God, I can feel a foot.
Double chins, well they're no-no's, but that doesn't worry me,
You see I stopped counting last week, when I found that I'd got three.
Tell me, why are models skinny when most of us are round?
And who'd want a spare rib, when steak comes by the pound.
Now sunbathing in a bikini, has long been a dream of mine,
But somewhere as I gained the weight, I lost my bikini line,
I'll admit my rear's a disgrace, and as a bottom, it should go,
They say it should be firm and high, mine's soft and hangs down low.
Models are flat-chested, when the opposite is me,
They strut the catwalk, topless, while I wear a double D.
Everything's a mismatch, *I'm voluptuous,* for goodness sake,
Oh now I've lost my urge for dieting, please just pass the wine and
                                        chocolate cake.

Pauline Daniels

A New Year Sandwich

Counting the year before
       the year after,

Could I say my life is
       at a standstill?

Marylène Walker

FORGIVENESS

Over the years, I have had family problems just like everyone else
most of them seem to occur once we get married.
In-laws appear to be the biggest problem
and every generation suffers just the same.
Daughter-in-law is not good enough for their son
son-in-law is not good enough for our daughter
he/she could have done better
and so it goes on.
Until one day when a small addition is made to the family.
Suddenly all the previous problems and heartaches disappear
and baby takes centre stage.
It seems quite strange that two people who are considered not good
enough for each other can produce a child and as if by magic,
everyone is happy and past feelings and differences are forgotten.
Maybe, we all try too hard to please one another.
Instead, we should all realise that we are all different and to try
and see each other's good points,
instead of always dwelling on one's bad points.
Only in times of grief do people seem to rally round and forget past
differences.
What a joy it would be if this were the norm,
if we could all live a happy and peaceful life together.
There but for the grace of God! go I, for none of us are saints.
Then we could all live a happy and peaceful life together.
Utopia, well maybe it is,
I have always been an optimist!
Just for once, let us all live together and to try and forgive and
forget our past failings.
Without relying on a grieving situation to become the glue that bonds
us together once again.
We may not always be able to forget,
but forgiveness is surely within everyone's heart.

David G Bennett

UNTITLED

God's forgiveness,
As readily available as an
Instant cup of coffee,
Can only be enlivening,
If drunk deeply and
'Taken on board'.

Gail

CLAIRE AND SHAY

Sitting outside Sainsbury's
With bundles of possessions,
Slight and boyish,
Dark braided hair beneath
Black baseball cap,
Black jacket, kneeless jeans
And trainers, she said,
'I'm Claire, and this
Is my husband, Shay.'

'We sleep in a tent,
In a field - we're lucky,
The farmer doesn't mind.'
I asked, 'Is it cold?'
Brightly she answered,
'No, we have our sleeping bags
And the tent traps the warmth,
Just like an igloo!
And Shay hopes to get a job,
Then we shall find
Somewhere to live.'

Her only concern was whether
I could manage to carry my
Shopping, on my bicycle.
'Be careful,' she said,
'Going round corners.'

I felt embarrassed and ashamed
Of having so much.
Humbled, I bore away my shopping.
God bless you,
Sweet, gallant Claire and Shay.

Maria-Christina

THE CHRISTMAS CARD

A Christmas card arrived today
One I had not really wanted
From a father long forgotten
Who'd scarred me deeply as a child.
Getting old his conscience pricked him
Thought he'd try to reconcile
All the hurts that lay between us
Parting us for many years.
Christmas time is for forgiveness
But is the power strong enough
To turn my feelings right around
When so unjustly I've been treated?
I've tried for years to just forget him
Pretended often he was dead
But now a card, he wants forgiveness
It's all been placed upon my head!
Who am I to sit in judgement?
Wrong I've done in my life too
But great the pain I still experience
When my thoughts to this man turn.
I can't forget the life he gave me
The consequences I fight each day
Making life an endless struggle
Where I could always sink or swim.
Perhaps we each must ask in turn
That we be forgiven from on high
For a past we cannot change now
But one with time we can let go.

Caroline Merrington

DISTANCES

Always reaching
Moving forward
Never touching
Pulling backward

These are distances.

Always speaking
Many phrases
Never listening
Pulling punches

These are distances.

Always telling
Many ideas
Never thinking
Pulling pints

These are distances.

Always knowing
Moving standpoints
Never settling
Pulling roots

These are distances.

Always fighting
Many issues
Never caring
Pulling rank

These are distances.

Always singing
Many lyrics
Never turning
Pulling audiences

Closing distances.

Paul Clissold

RECONCILIATION

In the world of good friends and relations
There's a widening gap of emotion
From hatred because of old history and slights
To excessive possessive devotion.

Where do you stand in this mixture of life
In the present or dogged by the past
Do you have courage to just be yourself
Make sure that past quarrels don't last?

So pick up the phone, write a letter
Inquire how they are, be a friend
Perhaps they'll be glad when they hear you
And to know that the feud's at an end.

If past actions were wounding and bitter
And your gesture they spurn and deride
Face up to your feeling and sadness
Don't be hurt, just remember you tried.

Enid Gill

DEAR SON

The yesterday years
that began to grow old
willingly and lovingly
with your birth, my son,
began to grow old willingly
and lovingly with the birth
of your sons my son.
The sad silent empty redundant years
that grow old without you, and your sons,
my son, grow old swiftly,
they float wastefully on the surface,
of a stagnant pool,
in a deep dark forest, with an empty tin,
and a phone, with an empty ring.
And the birthday card,
and the Christmas card, that never came.

Mam.

Babs Walters

IT'S HARD TO FORGET

It's hard to forget
Cast thoughts from your mind.
Harder to forgive
Those who are unkind.

What mother forgets a son
Whose life was sadly taken.
Can her life be the same?
As yet she breaths his name.

Friendship's a fragile thing
A joy when life is good.
Envy grown from selfishness
Destroys love and faithfulness.

There's always someone else to blame.
How can I be wrong?
Where is that truly perfect one?
We each have our shame.

Forgive them now. Don't wait.
Shed that grudge today.
Lest you find it's too late
The love has gone away.

Wendy Edwards

IT's ME WHO's DYING!

I should have let go.
This, I know.
After all of these years
of your rejections in my ears,
I should have let go because it's me who's dying!

I was worth so much more.
You were never satisfied.
I was never going to be my brother
who was more like you than I was.
I was worth so much more but now it's me who's dying!

I was never good enough for you.
You always put me down.
With every little quip and gibe
that stuck to my very being like mud.
I was never good enough for you, now it's me who's dying!

I have spent my whole life hating you.
You were proved wrong at death about me.
But everyone else said that I should forgive you
even though you never said 'Sorry!'
I have spent my whole life hating you, now it's me who's dying!

I've never got any peace with myself.
Whenever I think of you and what you did to me.
Seventy years have past but I still carry the scars
I should have let heal, but I see now it's been, by me holding on, that
I've never got any peace with myself;
and for years it's been me who's dying!

Philip Trivett

WHITE-OUT (SLIGHTLY WAN)

It was a 'white-out' Lord
When I heard you say:
'No-one dies on Christmas Day.'
You stripped me of sight,
And undressed me.
You shook me away from my family tree.

It was a 'white-out' Lord
On the second day.
Everyone had gone away.
I awoke at night
Disturbed in sleep
I couldn't get away from those patricide dreams.

It's a 'white-out' Lord,
No more stars in the sky.
Now I'm wishing I've a friend
Who has flowers in her eyes.
I have a seven-year itch.
My finger's on the trigger.
I'll aim my best, while sweating on the hammer.
And maybe your love
Is a bullet's kiss?
You'd better hope I'll miss.

Andrew John Elder

WATER UNDER THE BRIDGE

The hurt's so easy to inflict
Year through, unleashing torrents of ill-will;
Times when we never could predict
Regret that, through it all, we're loving still;
Bitterest battles start that way,
Emotions seething, to draw blood if need;
Hold out the hand of peace, I say;
The devil hovers but pay him no heed,
It's hard, like using damaged limb
Though tears of self-pity aren't far behind;
You chance a rebuff for this whim
But you will know then you tried to be kind
And you'll know that you chased away pain
That threatened with violence keen as a knife;
Make foe your friend, 'tis Yuletide again;
Than quarrels, my dear, there's much more to life.
It's strange that though we smart inside,
Shocked by unreasoning, terrible blow
To what we all have that's called 'pride',
Despite all, you just happen to know
Affection can blossom anew,
The tenderest, loveliest blessing there is;
Wayfarer, you know what to do -
Make no speeches nor crawl, offer that kiss!

Ruth Daviat

MY DAD

At one time he was to be trusted,
But never again I fear.
For he neglected us kids and Mummy,
And went off with his lover so dear.
He used to say that he loved us,
This was nothing but lies.
All he wanted was other women,
And they didn't make him wise.
Six weeks after he'd left us,
He regretted the decision he'd made,
And he came back to try and convince us,
That he really wished he had stayed.
We gave him another chance,
And forgave him for what he had done,
But a few months later, he'd had enough
And again was on the run.
We've heard nor seen of him since that day,
Now I doubt if we ever will,
But his conscience must prick him for
What he has done,
For he must remember us still.
Although it is hard to forgive him,
For treating his family so bad.
I simply cannot forget him
Because he is my *dad.*

It's 40 years since that fateful day
When first he went away
But the good things that he taught me then
Influence me today.

Pat Eppy

DREAM OF THE DEAD

I got back home in the early hours
of a cold, wet, lonely morning
and found my friend Jimmy leaning there
against the wall, though five years dead,
whole again now
and smiling his lopsided grin.

And we talked
because we two had walked through fires,
he my shadow and I his,
closer than lovers
in that ruin the guns had hacked at,
and all the things I could not say
to others, he knew already
and smiled, knowing.

Oh, that storm of blood! Oh, that harsh laughter!
How our horrified faces had ignited with disbelief!
How we had longed to say the simple things simply again
and could not find the way!

Now I asked him, how long
must I wage war with my disgust?
How long before I am whole again?
And even as his appearance faded
I heard a voice - it was his - say
holy
   in the name of humanity
when love has cast out hatred with its tears.

And I stepped after him one pace into eternity,
one pace before the spirit caught me,
knowing that this was Knowledge,
this was the Logos
and the sole End of man.

Colin Mackay

Questions For The Living

If you returned and heard I'd died.
What would the words that you denied me be?
What would you do to turn back time?
Saying no . . . no . . . she was mine.
You can't take her away!
What would the words that you would long so, to say to me?

Would they be . . . I loved you so?
Would they be, how could you go?
Would they be my darling friend, I,
will care for you until the end of time.
Would they be . . . I miss you so?
Would they be, how could you go?
I am sorry I did not tell you!

I believe in no regrets.
Time is short and builds up debts, we,
do not know we owe.
Until one says . . .
'Oh her, she died . . .
Such a shock . . . but time does fly . . .
It's the same for all of us.'

Sheila Mack

FORGIVE AND FORGET

The harsh word that cannot be retracted;
The unintentioned slight;
The silence that's enacted,
That burns and festers, try as one might

To wipe it from one's mind.
Imagined wrongs, blown up, dwelt upon,
From the word spoken, that's unkind,
The feelings that once were fond,

Can almost be erased.
Doubts and fears are sown,
On these thoughts are based.
Which we should disown.

If reconciliation is to follow,
An advantage is a short memory.
And if these words sound hollow,
The bad feeling is only temporary.

Life is short my friend,
Say those precious words now;
To your enemy make amend;
The first seeds you must sow.

An inner glow you will feel
That a wrong has been righted,
When rifts begin to heal,
No longer one feels slighted.

D A Dart

PEACE

You hurt me you know
Real damage
I thought I'd never recover
But it was years ago
And I've moved on
I hope I've changed
And that you have too
I don't have you anymore
Though it's taken time
But to reminisce now
(Without all the pain)
It's not the same
I was at fault
As much as you
Or maybe more
- Who knows
There's no pain left
The anger has gone
And if I saw you again
I wouldn't shout and scream
I'd just like you to know
I forgive you
(And I'm sorry.)

Monica Evans

FORGIVE . . . AND FORGIVE . . .

O Lord, help me learn to forgive . . .
And forget all the sins that I've done . . .
My Father, You know how I live -
I've not always loved like Your Son!
I've broken Your heart and done wrong -
I've fallen for Lucifer's lies . . .
I've chosen my own way so long,
I've nothing to offer but sighs . . .
I'm pleading Your pardon once more -
I'm asking for grace once again . . .
Forgive me for breaking Your Law . . .
I followed the ideas of men.
Excuses I needn't explain -
What use when the Lord is divine?
You've reason each time to complain -
You know that the faults are all mine!
O Lord, teach me wisdom always -
To help me to live life anew . . .
Such if I'm hurt by one who strays,
I've learnt to love mercy like You . . .

Denis Martindale

NOWHERE TO GO

I had it all at one time
A home and parents to
But things had changed
No more could I stand
The shouting and abuse
I packed my bags
And travelled
I felt I was no use
Little money do I have
I beg steal and borrow
If I could change my
Life around
I would go home tomorrow

Poet P M Wardle

FAMILY APART

The love in a family so far apart
Still holds close each in their heart
Distances miles kept near our sides
The words we are searching some of the lies

Hastening to push further and further
Away from the pain the hurt and the fervour
Said at the moment forgetting us all
Nobody thinking no one to call

Listening to others wedging apart
Sayings they say not from the heart
Rage will infest us love's thrown aside
Losing a loved one long is the ride

The hurt that we feel the pain and the cost
A family losing soon everything lost
Wider and wider the gap's getting out
The pain so heavy we all have to shout

Not one forgotten all talked about
All are remembered none put to rout
Loved as we are missed from the heart
Getting together first is the start.

John Barker

CURSES AT EASTER

Hanging back in the last pews out of sight.
Waiting to pounce like claws in dark night;
Stealing off with the collection box
Churlish as the chicken-stuffed fox!

Well - you piece of excretia
I would heap execrations upon you -
But mindful of Easter, Minister talks forgiveness.

So, remember, Christ hung between two such as you
And we don't know why you do what you do!
Son of God forgiving His thieves
And though you couldn't have stolen much -
Or even any because you dropped it -
You sullied this sanctity:
Another Easter point; Broken Temple.

And deep in thought I hate this time
Celebrating the death of a God who didn't do the crime

Oh, Angels in gardens
And stranger at Emmaus
Death defeated
Forgiveness and pardons
Adam's folly overthrown, Abba - hear us . . .

Suzanne Stratful

FORGIVE AND FORGET

The year dies; the earth is cold and bare
let not our hearts be cold as well.
There will be warmth, we shall be aware
of earth's Spring, and in our hearts let it dwell.

We have been wounded by a hasty word,
a thoughtless deed has left a bruising mark,
we have been saddened by something overheard,
stung to anger by a malicious remark.

Felt put upon, thought we've been ill-used,
lost our way in bitter argument,
felt furious when presented with the bill
why should we alone have to make the payment?

Clean your hearts of hatred and resentment
forget the stored-up wrongs; be not upset,
open your hearts, sit not in judgement,
forgive, forgive, and try, oh try to forget.

Marge Chamberlain

OUR FEUD GOES ON

Although, I was prepared to listen, let you have your say,
The ball was placed in your court but you did not want to play.
Surely now would be a good time to forgive and forget,
But it seems that you are still not ready to do this yet.
An apology for your actions would not be difficult,
Then harmony could be reached, leading to calm, a result.
However, you are proud, do not want to admit you're wrong,
In British tradition, stiff upper lip, our feud goes on.

Susan Mullinger

COMMUNION

Barriers are erected so thinly that strong
silver coated asbestos shield is needed to
protect the independent body, like a thong
made of smooth silk covering bones and spaces; brew
covers appear very firm, resisting dripping;
only dreams of independence flow out, spirit
disseminating as if from healthy gripping
properly layered pink skin. Unmoved mover move it!
Restore, create flush to skin and bone, without which
poisoned, as legendary legion shifter, witch
hunt drowned poor pigs - healed man open to Kingdom.
As the Sower produces risen bread - best wine, -
quantum leap of faith enables me and you to shine.

Robert D Shooter

THE APOLOGY

If I were you
Then I would be
pretty peeved and mad at me
If you were me
what would you do
would you apologise to you?
I do.

Pippa Farina

I WILL . . .

This year I vow to eat less chocolate,
All my clothes this year *shall* fit.
I'll drink less wine and spirits and beer,
I *will* reduce the size of my rear.

I'll never tell fibs or even white lies,
And the size of my ego will reduce in size.
I'll be honest and innocent, pure and sweet,
My handwriting will always be tidy and neat.

I'll be efficient and organised in everything I do,
I'll tidy the kitchen and bathroom too.
I'll plan out my year, month, week and my day,
I'll watch every sentence and word I say.

These are my resolutions for '99,
Whether I stick to them depends on time,
So come back and ask me this time next year,
The answer will probably be *No!*, I fear.

Julie Dawn Coventry

GRANNY'S MILLENNIUM CHANGE

Granny's millennium change
Was to carefully arrange
Some red and yellow flowers we sent her
From the garden centre.
They went with her forty-year-old bulrushes
To make some lovely, colourful touches.

Claudia Miller-Williams

RESOLUTIONS

The same 'old' promise, 'new' each year.
I'll give up spirits, wines and beer.
I'll cut out fags, stop eating meat.
These awful habits I shall beat.

Then dawns the second day of May.
(I'm sixty two this very day.)
I pour a drink to celebrate,
And roll a fag, and seal my fate.

Then to the local pub I walk
For a slap-up meal, five veg, and pork.
And then I wash it down, oh dear!
Ten pints of local bitter beer.

Resolution up the spout,
Again it's meat and beer and 'snout'.
I'd like to make it very clear,
I'll do it all again

Next year!

A Gifford

RESOLUTIONS

Moving places - moving rooms
What do I do with all of my things
Do a clear-out and you will have room
Don't be so lazy to keep yourself busy

After you're done
You'll look all around
And say to yourself
My mum I feel proud
To have been able
To make my room clean

Moving places - moving rooms

Ann Buchanan

Typhoo - O - Tabooed

I have been told so many times,
Too much is not good for me.
And I have tried so many times,
To cut down on the tea.

If I hid the teapot,
Would it work for me?
I doubt it, for the spoons and mugs,
Would say 'Have a cup of tea?'

Have a little willpower,
Erase it from your mind.
But this begins to suffer,
When friends call in I find.

The tray is laid, the kettle on,
We sit by the fire and chat,
Good intentions have all gone,
And that's the end of that.

Drink more water, that is cold,
Warmth is needed when getting old,
I've yet to find the answer,
How can I refrain,
My former resolutions have
All gone down the drain.

F L Brain

MOMENTS IN HAIKU

Sand in an hourglass
A universe in each grain
Spiralling through time

Your life in one day
Epoch of brilliant change
Dragonfly envy

Glyphs on a headstone
Eighty summers span two dates
And what did you learn?

Seasons, tick, sundial
Eternity of shadows
Dandelion clocks chime

Candlelight vigil
Breath impaled on icy glass
Only moths feed flames

Face in a mirror
Frozen forever in time
Between each new line

Barbara L Richards

TICK

The yellow clock tocks
proudly loud this rainy day
must I take its life?

Debbie Charles

THE ANSWER I WILL NEVER KNOW

Alone am I, walking the streets of the town where I was born,
The people I meet are all strangers to me
Gone are the faces I once knew;
Even the ground beneath my feet is foreign to me
Gone is the smell of tar, and the men whom once did lay the
tar-covered stones
And the 'puff, puff, puff' . . . of the steamroller as it rolled
O'er the tar-covered stones, making the surface o' so smooth
In its place, bricks . . . laid to a pattern, very neat . . . but why?
Traffic no longer is allowed an entry . . .
'Pedestrians only' . . . as they promenade in their hundreds
'Shop window gazing' . . . wherever the money comes from I do
not know . . .
But somehow it is found . . . 'A far cry from my day'.

Many are the years has my life's traversed,
Most of the time, looking for work, but rarely lucky enough to find
Still I kept a smile upon my face . . . to those I met -
And those friends I knew, I would stop . . . just to have a word, or two;
There were the times, I've cursed, asking myself . . . 'Why was
I born at all?'
That was the time I cursed, puzzling my brain, wondering,
Was it true love? Or, did Mother fall . . . for Father's charm?
Not knowing the answer was the reason for my cursing.

Here I am, alone in this world, have been for many years
A world, so sordid, many are deprived of a home -
And food are they denied, left to roam without shelter,
Whilst a cardboard box to suffice for a bed . . . in some shop doorway;
Still, it is not the world itself to blame . . . o' no,
'Tis many of those whom live within it, my mind is in turmoil
Wondering . . . why was I born? If only I knew the answer,
Was it true love, or just Father's charm?
Damn it! The answer I will never know.

Leslie F Dukes

WHEN THE BULLETS CAME

It is said when the bullets came
Mothers did not cry rivers of streaking rain
But from the leaking wounds of their bodies blood came

It is sworn children did not instinctively scream their mothers' names
Instead they crowded under their bedcovers in ruthless forces of pain

It is said when the bullets came
The bodies of fathers blurred into shock leaving them to become fragile
and lame
None were able to reach for the committed gun that many a time before
had been used to main
But all the same
Their quivering bones pierced in anguish
Smashing down upon the cursed landscape where they attempted to
defend the lives that are now so drained

It is said when the bullets came
The cradle holding the baby no longer rocked back and forth
The classroom no longer seated an enthusiastic pupil at each of its
accompanying desk
And the exhibited windows created the atmosphere of the deserted
workplace
Giving the impression it had been closed for the weekend rest
But the once crowded streets they did look in mourning all lost in
loneliness

It is said when the bullets came
There was no time for proud men to wear army suits or carry guns
There was no time to form vigilante groups to patrol the streets run
There was time and time only for dying

Saheeda Khan

MINNOWS IN A MILL POND

Minnows in a mill pond, no movement, so serene
Not a care to haunt them, hidden behind a screen
No turning wheels to deafen - life goes gently by
But those in the fast lane, in that flowing stream
Never had the privilege - and never had a dream

Minnows in a flowing river - wider now and rough
Predators hunting their prey, doesn't life get tough
Oh, to be in that mill pond, swimming at their ease
Nothing now to frighten them, just a croaking frog
Leaping oh so merrily - across the floating log

But fortune only favours those brave and bold
Being a minnow in a stream - rushing sharp 'n' cold
No place for the timid - for out there in the sea
Sharks as big as mountains - will be after thee
Stay put little minnow - enjoy the prize of life

Robert Jennings-McCormick

WORLD OF CHANGE

What's happened to the
'turning' of the seasons,
- it would appear -
- gone are those, -
that we knew, of yesterday.

Flood waters burst from the river
banks, no longer imprisoned,
the sun's scorching heat brings
tears to the ice flow,
have we destroyed by the
intelligence of our own ignorance,
the world we all, so once loved to know.

Has the almighty in his wisdom,
withdrawn his gifts - which were
never for sale,
and those who chose to abuse
his creations,
now find themselves in the
position, of having the price
of his bill to pay.

Let's hope - that the lesson -we
chose not to learn,
will be heeded by the 'young' of today,
and that it isn't too late - and we
haven't ruined forever,
'the world' - which as a gift -
to each and everyone of us
he gave.

Bakewell Burt

HOT-WATER BOTTLE

My feet are cold I don't want to get up
Not even for 'chocolate' to sup.
My feet can't cope, it's cold in here
I am sincere.

A water bottle is the answer I feel
But I have no zeal.
Water bottle, cold feet, what is the answer?
Your feet are cold, you're no longer a dancer.

You need courage to get out of bed
Come lift up your head.
The feet will follow as you go to the tap,
As you bring back your hot-water bottle wearing your wrap.

Denise Shaw

To The Loch Ness Monster

Deep, deep, deep she lays
This ancient serpent of
The loch
With crested head and jagged
Jaw this beast that time repented
For.
With stature mighty as
A house and nature timid
As a mouse this lonely
Creature that time forgot
This dinosaur that
Haunts the loch

David A Bray

A ROYAL CHRISTMAS PRESENT

A proud Norwegian has just arrived -
a veritable queen
or evergreens
- to reign
in the heart of this big town
- an inspiring sight!
It is so lofty and handsome - full of poise and charm.
With its wide branches, stretching like arms,
is keen to put in a festive spirit not only Londoners,
but anyone who passes by
the famous Square with Nelson perched up on high.
Yet there's more than meets the eye.
For that Christmas tree is there to signify
that 'it's the season of giving and sharing,'
as it is a royal gift in itself,
from Norway to the UK
for giving his hand
to free it from the throes of peril
in the dark days.
Besides that imposing foreigner
is here to symbolise
a determination and courage of its small country today
to stand bravely alone outside
the EU, and never waver nor to be afraid.
For independence is the only way
to make one survive and thrive,
grow stronger all the time -
an example to follow for us all.
Come along folks, welcome to this town
to revel in front of the wonderful fir tree
exuding the scent of freedom
- to celebrate Christmastime
- to find out how to cherish freedom
  as the most precious thing in life!

Lucy Carrington

A Treasure Chest

I have a chest of treasured joys abounding
Wherein, lie golden gifts of yore, enhancing
The silver notes of August, now resounding
To greet the autumn breeze, - advancing

See thro' the gleam, a saffron morn, emerging,
A boy: maternal heart and hand entwining,
Cast leaven crusts to dappled ducklings surging,
Fluff-winged, across mottled mere - bright shining.

The bitter tang of woodsmoke gently curling,
Aloft, a hovering lark is singing,
Come: drink the scent of hyacinth unfurling -
Bluebells, - a zephyr's touch sets ringing.

Cream claret tramcars - market shopping,
Nice things . . .
A sallow leaf, and polished chestnuts dropping,
A hint that summer's reign is ending.

Trevor Woodhead

SUBMISSIONS INVITED
SOMETHING FOR EVERYONE

POETRY NOW '99 - Any subject,
any style, any time.

WOMENSWORDS '99 - Strictly women,
have your say the female way!

STRONGWORDS '99 - Warning!
Age restriction, must be between 16-24,
opinionated and have strong views.
(Not for the faint-hearted)

All poems no longer than 30 lines.
Always welcome! No fee!
Cash Prizes to be won!

Mark your envelope (eg *Poetry Now*) *'99*
Send to:
Forward Press Ltd
Remus House, Coltsfoot Drive
Woodston, Peterborough
PE2 9JX

OVER £10,000 POETRY PRIZES
TO BE WON!

Judging will take place in October 1999